Roadrunners

by Megan Borgert-Spaniol

BLASTOFF! READERS

BELLWETHER MEDIA · MINNEAPOLIS, MN

Note to Librarians, Teachers, and Parents:

Blastoff! Readers are carefully developed by literacy experts and combine standards-based content with developmentally appropriate text.

Level 1 provides the most support through repetition of high-frequency words, light text, predictable sentence patterns, and strong visual support.

Level 2 offers early readers a bit more challenge through varied simple sentences, increased text load, and less repetition of high-frequency words.

Level 3 advances early-fluent readers toward fluency through increased text and concept load, less reliance on visuals, longer sentences, and more literary language.

Level 4 builds reading stamina by providing more text per page, increased use of punctuation, greater variation in sentence patterns, and increasingly challenging vocabulary.

Level 5 encourages children to move from "learning to read" to "reading to learn" by providing even more text, varied writing styles, and less familiar topics.

Whichever book is right for your reader, Blastoff! Readers are the perfect books to build confidence and encourage a love of reading that will last a lifetime!

This edition first published in 2014 by Bellwether Media, Inc.

No part of this publication may be reproduced in whole or in part without written permission of the publisher. For information regarding permission, write to Bellwether Media, Inc., Attention: Permissions Department, 5357 Penn Avenue South, Minneapolis, MN 55419.

Library of Congress Cataloging-in-Publication Data

Borgert-Spaniol, Megan, 1989- author.
  Roadrunners / by Megan Borgert-Spaniol.
     pages cm. – (Blastoff! Readers. Backyard Wildlife)
  Summary: "Developed by literacy experts for students in kindergarten through grade three, this book introduces roadrunners to young readers through leveled text and related photos"– Provided by publisher.
  Audience: 5 to 8
  Audience: K to grade 3.
  Includes bibliographical references and index.
  ISBN 978-1-62617-061-2 (hardcover : alk. paper)
  1. Roadrunner–Juvenile literature. I. Title. II. Series: Blastoff! readers. 1, Backyard wildlife.
  QL696.C83B67 2014
  598.7'4–dc23
                                 2013032360

J598.7
BOR

Printed in the United States of America, North Mankato, MN.

Contents

Roadrunners are birds with long legs and tails. They live in **deserts** and dry grasslands.

Roadrunners have a **crest** of black feathers. They raise it when they are upset.

crest

Roadrunners do not like to fly. They **sprint** along the ground instead.

Their tails help them **steer** and stop.

Roadrunners chase **insects**, lizards, and **rodents**. Sometimes they grab small birds from the air.

Roadrunners also attack dangerous snakes. They whack their **prey** against the ground.

Roadrunners watch out for hawks, coyotes, and raccoons. They can fly to escape these **predators**.

Roadrunners build nests for their eggs. They use sticks, grasses, and feathers.

Both parents keep the eggs warm in the nest. Soon chicks burst out of the eggs!

Glossary

crest—a group of feathers on the heads of some birds

deserts—dry lands with little rain

insects—small animals with six legs and hard outer bodies; insect bodies are divided into three parts.

predators—animals that hunt other animals for food

prey—animals that are hunted by other animals for food

rodents—small animals with front teeth that grow throughout life; rats, mice, and squirrels are types of rodents.

sprint—to run very fast for a short time

steer—to turn in different directions

To Learn More

AT THE LIBRARY

Ganeri, Anita. *Roadrunner.* Chicago, Ill.: Heinemann Library, 2011.

Schuetz, Kari. *Birds.* Minneapolis, Minn.: Bellwether Media, 2013.

Storad, Conrad J. *Lizards for Lunch: A Roadrunner's Tale.* El Cajon, Calif.: Sunbelt Publications, 2002.

ON THE WEB

Learning more about roadrunners is as easy as 1, 2, 3.

1. Go to www.factsurfer.com.

2. Enter "roadrunners" into the search box.

3. Click the "Surf" button and you will see a list of related Web sites.

With factsurfer.com, finding more information is just a click away.

Index

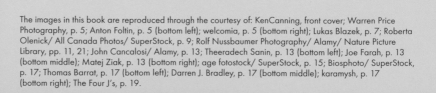

The images in this book are reproduced through the courtesy of: KenCanning, front cover; Warren Price Photography, p. 5; Anton Foltin, p. 5 (bottom left); welcomia, p. 5 (bottom right); Lukas Blazek, p. 7; Roberta Olenick/ All Canada Photos/ SuperStock, p. 9; Rolf Nussbaumer Photography/ Alamy/ Nature Picture Library, pp. 11, 21; John Cancalosi/ Alamy, p. 13; Theeradech Sanin, p. 13 (bottom left); Joe Farah, p. 13 (bottom middle); Matej Ziak, p. 13 (bottom right); age fotostock/ SuperStock, p. 15; Biosphoto/ SuperStock, p. 17; Thomas Barrat, p. 17 (bottom left); Darren J. Bradley, p. 17 (bottom middle); karamysh, p. 17 (bottom right); The Four J's, p. 19.